The Unnoticeable HEART

WENDY SIMS

ISBN 979-8-89043-065-6 (paperback)
ISBN 979-8-89043-066-3 (digital)

Christian Faith Publishing
832 Park Avenue
Meadville, PA 16335
www.christianfaithpublishing.com

Printed in the United States of America

CONTENTS

INTRODUCTION

In the 1970s, families never talked about certain things that may have happened inside their circles. They were to remain as if they never happened. This was my family. Hello, my name is Wendy Sims, and this is a true story of my life from infancy to childhood and then from a teen to an adult. The secrets were kept, silenced, and denied until the times of today. It's a bit awkward, such things as abuse and trauma; even rape is a secret never told in society. It was a way of life that was never taught differently, and I was too scared to say anything for fear of retaliation.

There were threats against my life, and I felt trapped in the situation for a long time. According to *Britannica*, the definition of *child abuse*, also called *cruelty to children*, is the willful infliction of pain and suffering on children through physical, sexual, or emotional mistreatment. Prior to the 1970s, the term *child abuse* normally referred to only physical mistreatment, but since then, its application has expanded to include, in addition to inordinate physical violence, unjustifiable verbal abuse; the failure to furnish proper shelter, nourishment, medical treatment, or emotional support; incest and other cases of sexual molestation or rape; and the use of children in prostitution or pornography.

According to Childhelp, every year, more than four million referrals are made to child protection agencies involving more than 4.3 million children. In today's society, it is well-known what child abuse is. This is a recurring situation in its own field that never ends. Most abusers were abused, but some are just cruel by nature and thrive on controlling and hurting others.

My mother was not abused in her life, but she was a narcissist in every way. I always believed she was schizophrenic because of the way she would act. I knew for a fact she was a narcissist because of the control factor and the verbal, mental, and physical abuse.

My mother was my abuser and the evilest person I ever met on earth. Today I have not spoken to her in at least fourteen or more years. My life has been so much better without her in it. I know she is still mean. The type of woman that when she looked at me, I could just see the evil in her eyes and on her face. She was like Dr. Jekyll and Mr. Hyde. She can smile and make herself look like an angel, and people would fall for her schemes.

This story is about my life, the trials I had to go through, and the physical and emotional pain. There are just some people in this world you cannot change, but you must do your best to live your life and survive. To look through the eyes of the person, you must see the true life bestowed upon them and not the fake smiles and happiness. Knowing the truth does set you free in an era of no mistaken anger, pain, and hate.

As you read this story, I hope that you can see how strong the spirit can be and how hard it can be to break it. Knowing survival and submission and the difference between them in life itself, the soul and spirit can survive through anything they are put through.

CHAPTER 1

The Beginning

I Was Yours

I do not know why you received me
For when the time came
I was conceived
And there was supposed to be joy and love
You could not think of any above
As a child, I wished and prayed
I just didn't understand why
I had to stay
When I looked at you
The anger and distaste
Like I was just a waste
I tried so hard to please you
No matter what I did, I did not complete you
I only wanted your love
But you only would give me shame
The more I tried
The more I died
A heart of a child
Reaching out to you
But you just refused
You hit, you cut
This little child
Like the devil in you
Tormenting, gnashing, and gashing
The soul and the flesh
Joy in the bashing
Why such torture
To such innocence
Why not just finish it?
A slave for always
In the days to come
A savior there?

No not one
A child's soul lost
A child's love couldn't be bought
Living in chains
Flesh, soul, and heart
Couldn't show the shame
There was no game
Loss of love and pride in you
That no one can renew

Every day, there is a miracle, no matter what it is. There are small and big miracles in the world that people never seem to notice. So many things pass us by, and we just look past them. There is one miracle that you cannot ignore, and that is when God gives life. The life that is created between a man and a woman is just a miracle in itself. To become a life and grow inside a woman's womb is such a life-changing experience. To find out that you have a life growing inside you can be an awesome life-changing event. To some, it is a miracle, and to some, a burden.

On January 6, 1976, a little girl was born. This little life was God's creation and meant to be treasured in all things. She was born to a mother, who already had two children and was married to a man, her husband and partner. Little did this child know what she was about to be born into and the circumstances around her life: a mother who had no more regard for herself nor any of her children. As the days came and went, the child grew and understood. The child was me.

Being locked in the room as a child, she would leave us children in the home by ourselves. I was growing up not knowing why she seemed to hate me so much. When she looked at me, I could see the regret and hatred. I waited for her to say, "I love you," but it never came. Life was dressed as fear for not knowing what would become of me. I came into a life where I could do nothing right in her eyes. Remembering myself as a small child, I just wanted to stay in school and never come home.

I was trapped. I was not safe, but I could not get away. Most of my memories as a child are sad. I do not remember any good times. When I was away from my mom, I remember feeling kind of safe. I could tell she wished she had never had me. She had the same look toward my sister. The distaste she had for us girls was intense, but not for her son, who was an angel in her eyes.

I can remember the way he could get away with anything. I remember a time when my mom put me in a chair in front of the stove and lit the top burner. As a child, I thought we were going to cook, but to my surprise, she grabbed my hand and put it over the fire. The smell of my searing flesh was like something I can't describe in words. It was worse than a dog that was dead for several days on the road. The pain! As the flame hit my skin, I could feel it start to fry. Screaming at the top of my lungs, I tried to get away but couldn't. My sister ran in and hit our mother on the side so she would let go of me. My sister then took me in her arms, ran, and hid with me. I never wanted to see my mom again and did not understand what I could have done at three years old to deserve such a punishment.

Even as a child, I saw my mom as evil. To survive, I had to forget what happened and hide it in the back of my mind, blocking the incident and not thinking of it again. We moved from house to house. I remember living in a two-story house, and the top floor was where my sister and I would play. The only good memories I have were those times with my sister. We would play for hours up there, and I never wanted to leave. It was my world away from evil and pain. The floor below was where the bruises and welts were imprinted on my body and skin.

A child's innocence was torn and beaten out, only knowing the life of shame. Being told as a child that "you are not worth the air you are breathing" brought sadness and confusion about why I deserved to be born. To be told, "I should have never had you," was so cruel to my heart. Sometimes I would wish I were not born and that God would just take me. To see my mom be so sweet to my brother and wondering why she was not that way with me and my sister tortured my soul and mind, and I could not dream or have a child's joy.

Always doing what she wanted around the house still did not satisfy her. No one was there to save me or rescue me from her grasp and mind control. As a child reaching out to her, she never reached back. She was like a soulless evil flesh of a human. The way she would look at me as a child would make you cringe. Not realizing as a child that I was being brainwashed and abused in every way possible, I just thought that this was my life and that was how it was. I tiptoed around trying to please her in every way possible, but I never knew what the results of my actions would be.

The feeling of not being loved and wanted as a child struck me like lightning in a storm, hitting a pole and ripping it in half. Imagine taking your heart from your chest and squeezing it tightly in your hand until you just can't feel it anymore. Now imagine doing that to a child who only has love and innocence to be given and to have. Looking from the outside, you would think I was a happy child, but from the inside, I couldn't tell you what I was. The child within me was just there, dying little by little and screaming for help, but no one could hear me. So why I was born in this world as a child I could not understand, and the pain in my life I could not express.

CHAPTER 2

Child's Eyes

Sister

The fun and joy with you
The things we would do
I was happy while you were there
As we sat in the chair
Laughter, love, and life
You could take away my strife
My hero in my eye
You could never die
My savior my friend
You were there till the end
The day you were taken away
I so prayed
I lost my friend
That I could not pretend
As it became harder with you gone
I was forever alone
In my dreams of you coming back
Just to take me with you just like that
Seeing that smile
As I ran for miles
Wishing to God to see you again
Was a dream over again
But always, the dream would end
Praying one day
To see your face
Just so my heart can smile again
Never forgetting my hero
Though the chances of seeing you again were zero

To have a sister as a child was the most wonderful experience. She was my hero in many ways. I think that if it was not for her in my childhood, I would have been gone a long time ago. Being able to play with her was like heaven on earth. She was my Wonder Woman. Since she went through what I did, she knew how I felt as a child. She saved me many times, held me, and told me it would be okay. She was so beautiful to me like an angel in the sky. I remember us playing in our playroom with dolls, and I saw the same pain in her eyes that I had in mine. We were in the same boat, trying to paddle far away. Then one day, she was rescued, and there she was no more. The day she left was the day I died even more. I was happy that she was rescued and could live a safe life now. I was sad, though, knowing I would probably never see her again. My heart cracked a little more. My love for her was always there, and I prayed every night that she could feel it. I prayed as a child that I would see her again so I could have the courage to live.

As the days got longer, I slowly started to realize she would not be back. My heart ached, and it left a hole that was never filled. I knew that she probably thought of me, and I prayed that I would see her one day. I tried to be brave, but it was never the same. After her father's family took her, my life became even worse. My mother beat me more and did more things that I thought a mother could never do to a child. I think she was angry because my sister was not there, so she directed that rage at me like it was somehow my fault.

I always thought about my sister and wondered what her life was like, what she looked like, and if she ever thought of me. I knew she would be a beautiful person, and she was always smart. So even though she was not there physically, she was always a part of my life. I would imagine her and what she would look like in my mind as a child. I know that was a part of what kept me going and praying one day my dreams would come true. One day, we would find each other again, and it would be as if we never parted.

Don

I can only describe my feelings
Through a revealing poem
So this one's for you
It's the best I can do!

I have so many feelings
I don't know which one is which
I don't know which one
Is more crushing to
My heart because of you
There is so much pain
But so much more to gain
If only it could be true
How could you deny me?
And not try to find me?
To see if I am truly yours
When I was a child
I was meek and mild
But now I am grown
I can take care of my own
But I always needed you too!
But you said I was not yours
Was there not an intercourse
With a woman?
But yet you said, "No way"
However, it is true
Happy days, in fact, all the days
You have missed them, everyone
Where was your courage?
I was the one left
Trying to love you
Throughout life, I've had pain
What was there to gain, surely not you!

My mom and dad didn't stay together. They got divorced, and he left. Just to add more pain and more scars, I do not remember him visiting very often as a child. I do remember a time he came and left, and then we never saw him again. I know he worked a lot, and she left a lot. When he left, it just chipped away more of the hole I had already. Not hearing from him and wondering why he left me with her, I couldn't understand the reasoning behind it. She had no pictures on the wall of me, my dad, or any of us. She was so cruel.

I remember her saying that my dad didn't want us and that he was a deadbeat. She also told me that he hated us and that we would never see each other again because he didn't care about us. Hearing this over and over as a kid, I believed it. There were no phone calls or letters. He just vanished like a ghost. I thought about him all the time. I wondered what I did that made him leave. Why did he not take me with him when he knew how mean she was?

I was told as a small child that she had left us locked in the room of the house, but the front door was unlocked. My grandpa told me the story of how he walked into the house to find no one there. My grandpa unlocked the bedroom door and found my brother on the floor, playing with his toys, and me in the crib. He said that I had ants all over me because I had a dirty diaper, and the ants were biting me all over. Grandpa called my dad, and he came home and saw it, and all Grandpa said was, "Everything hit the fan."

As a child, I always thought it was my fault that he left. I had no one to tell me otherwise. I hoped that if I was good enough for my mom, then he would come back, get me, and take me with him. Being told as a child that my dad was saying I was not his child even pushed the knife in deeper. Not having my dad broke me as I got older. He missed all the important days. He did not see me mature into a young woman, and he missed the birthdays and Christmases. There were no phone calls or anything. It was as if I never existed. I felt as if I was just made to be given away just so they could say I was theirs.

As years passed, he married and had other stepchildren, but he never tried to find me, as if I were never born. I would see kids at school with their dads, and I would just cry because he was not there.

There was never a father-daughter dance or a father to watch me when I graduated from school. But there was so much of something else—so much pain and heartache. Once again, there was the feeling that I was not wanted.

Can You Hear Me?

Where are you?
Can you hear me?
Like silence upon dew
My heart cries out
My soul is torn
I can't shout
The tears flow down
A drop at a time
My knees hit the ground
The more they come sliding down
The river flows
I call your name
Jesus, God
I can't hear anything
I try to talk to you
The best I can
What more can I do?
I feel so alone
Tattered and worn
Am I on my own?
Tell me what matters
Torn, beaten, and bruised
What is there left to gather?
Do you hear my cry?
Do you hear?
Can you feel my soul die?
I'm in so much pain
Head, heart, and flesh
What else can I contain?
I ask in your name
Save me if you hear
Or let me just burst into flames

I prayed, not knowing where God had gone. I believed that he had left me and didn't care. I got to the point where I couldn't shout his name or even say it because of the pain in my heart and soul. It felt like I was on a roller coaster going round and round, constantly crying in silence and asking, "Why me?" and receiving no peace. All the pain in my flesh was just there, and it was not going anywhere. My heart told me one thing, and the voices in my head told me another, like an internal war constantly raging. The loneliness that I felt in my heart and soul was so overwhelming that my body just gave in. If he did not hear me then, why wouldn't he just let me burst into pieces and leave the earth?

My Life

I sit here, thinking about life
What it means to live
I pray at the end of the day, which we call the night
But it seems every day that I hope and pray
Nothing gets any better
I can't say it in a letter
I think of the years that have passed by
I can't remember any of the real good times
Except for the love of a hero sister
There is no doubt about that
But now, where am I at?
Now that I sit down and think
I wonder if I should be buried deep
I feel as if someone has a knife to my back
Who is turning it without no slack
The pain that flows through me
It feels so real, so deep that my heart
Gives up and surrenders to the pain that makes me weep
I feel as if I am a failure
That I cannot do anything right
I can't take it anymore, so I guess
I will just give up the fight
This world can be so cruel
It's like everyone is trying to rule
My life is so unhappy
That I can hear everyone laughing
I cry and weep at night
It seems I can't stop the fight
So what am I to do with this life?
Should I go on or say good night?

My life has been one dark time, filled with hatred and depression, and overall, I just wanted to end my life altogether. Darkness begins to shade the sky, and as I pray, I wonder whether I am worth being heard. Everything just keeps getting worse.

I know I have had some love in my life, and I know that is one of the things that has kept me going. My memory evades me because I do not want to remember all the bad times. I do not remember any good times except for two: with my stepdad who actually treated me like his own and with my sister. What I do remember the most is my body aching in pain and hurts and my soul being in the deepest hole there could be. I thought of just lying down and going to sleep and never waking up, wanting to give up on everything in my life as I had no hope to spare. I watched others so happy and wondered, *Why? Why can I not be happy?* Seeing people laugh at me added to the shame already in me. The fight left me, and I was just breathing flesh. I cried every night in bed, wishing someone would just rescue me or for me to just never breathe again.

The pain my heart felt in my chest ached through the flesh of my body. Each morning, I dreaded walking out of my room. I knew evil was coming, and I felt unable to fight anymore.

How does a child fight with only what a child knows? People can be so cruel and think they have to rule everything. That same control that empowers some people to feel invincible causes its victims to lose themselves. I couldn't figure out where my life would go or what would become of me. Oh, how I wish I could see a better future, if I even had one. The more I tried to think, the worse the voices that had control in my head became, causing depression and a withdrawal from myself and everyone else. So I wore a fake smile like a mask to hide the pain, acting as if everything was okay when, in truth, my world was insane.

CHAPTER 3

Scars of the Soul

My Loving Child

Such a delightful soul
To be born in this world
That beautiful smile
So everlasting
To grow so wise
In such little time.
The kindest spirit
There is nothing near it
Whose belief has grown through thick or thin
Who seems to have made such fast mends
A survivor
Who can compare to no other
A soldier
Who now lets God hold her
As we know you are not far apart
You will always be close to the heart
As we say farewell and not goodbye
May you only have love and peace
In your heavenly life.

Dedicated to a special friend Angela Davis

What can I say about Angela Davis? What can I not say about her? She was a dear friend, and she always lent an ear. She had such a soft soul and was wise. She was the rock that helped me see some light in life. She could be tough as nails or soft as an angel, but she was always a true friend. I realize now that God sent her into my life at the time I needed her. She was my strength and my heart's healer. We used to talk so much, and I really enjoyed just being around her. She was an awesome friend and confidante. She was my shoulder to cry on, my listener, and my encourager. I was so sad when God took her home. I thought I was being punished for having such a good friend. She is so deeply missed by everyone. Seeing the smile on her face, even though it was not a good day or something was wrong, was so encouraging. You are still missed and loved, my friend.

The Night Flight

As day turns into night
My mind takes flight
As you squeeze the air from me
To wish you were done with me
Awaken to pain and blood
Flowing from my veins
Crying tears from my eyes
Wishing only to die
Wiping the red stains
To try to repair
The not knowing why
And only to collide
Not having any pride
So scared and wondering if I really died
Seeing imprints on my neck
But not really wanting to check
The loss of all life
To only know I have strife
Looking at what used to be me
And what must be a dream
The darkness in your eyes
The hatred inside
As you look into my eyes
Seeing you are not whole
Looks as if you have the devil's soul
So will this be the last time
That you climb on top of me in the night?
Squeeze the air out of me so tight?
What will be your shame?
When will there be a cleaning rain?

I never knew what would set her off and why she would do the things she did, which made my life hell on earth. She would get so mad and just go off. At this time, I had a nerve disease called RSD. It was nothing to play with, and it would paralyze whichever limb it was in if it reached the fourth stage. By the time they diagnosed me, I was in the third stage. I was hit above my temple, which was what caused the disease. It was on the left side of my face, left arm, and spine. I was in constant pain, and my limbs would go numb, and I could not feel at all. All I could feel when I started numbing was a tingling sensation.

She did not care about what I was going through, and she actually saw it as an advantage to get away with more torture. My mom would grab me around my throat with both hands and choke me out. I gasped and tried to fight with the one good arm I had. It was frightening to know she had such strength and hatred for me. I would wish she would just finish me off as it happened, but she didn't just so she could do it again. When I would wake up, I would either have bruises where she hit me with her fist or something else. Or I would wake up to cuts all over and blood running down. I would have to try to get up and get to the bathroom, which took all I had within me just to move. Not having discovered faith in God by that time in my life, when I awakened to such horrors, I wondered why I couldn't have just died in my sleep.

As she looked into my eyes, I could see the evil and darkness. She smiled like she was enjoying it. From the time when everything was going black to my sudden awakening, I would have had no awareness of how much time had passed. My neck felt like her hands were still around me and choking me. I didn't want to look in the mirror because I could feel what she had done. I felt the shame she inflicted on me from her hatred, but I could not understand where it came from.

I spent so much time crying for God to make it stop and trying to hide what she had done before I had to go to work (and yes, I went to work no matter what). If I had not worked, we would have been out on the street because she didn't want to work. I paid all the bills and her car insurance. Trying to hide everything was horrible.

Coming up with excuses all the time for why I was wearing some-thing or hurting when I tried doing something else was very hard. I just knew this was my life, and it would never change!

Lost Soul

Time to turn in
Such a long day
As the night falls
There is no pause
My eyes close
To no more light
Hear a noise
In the dark night
As a weight upon me
I can't move
I feel a tug to awaken me
To evil upon me
I can't call out
A hand over my mouth
Hearing, tearing, and gnashing
Feeling the groping
Tears flowing down my face
The evil upon me
Laughing and moaning
Asking God to take me now
Feeling myself fading
The evil inside me causes such pain
I know I had nothing remaining
The life sucked out of me
My soul was gone
Trying to fight, but I didn't win that night
The smile on your face
As you took my innocence
My life, my happiness
Powerless looking at you
The girl who once was is gone now
Wishing you were through

Begging you, God, to take my life
And leave me to die
The laughter, the evil
The glimmer in your eye
The satisfaction of taking my pride
You walking away, feeling accomplished
Taking my life as your conquest
The innocent life you took that night
Never again stayed
The life you took hers always
Had been shaken and never again regained
Never back or cut any slack
The soul taken
Was not mistaken
The night claimed the soul
The rest of the days
I just couldn't ever get away
I lost my soul that day

I never saw it coming, and when it did, the life that I once had was gone. What do you say? At the age of sixteen, I was raped by the brother of my mom's boyfriend, and he took my innocence and virginity. I never thought my life could get any worse, but I was wrong.

We lived with my mom's boyfriend, and his brother had come in from California and was staying there. He had a girlfriend, but they had broken up, and she left and went back to California. I really didn't like him too much and stayed away from him. He had been doing drugs and no telling what else in California, and he came to live with his brother. He came to start over and get away from the drugs, but I could tell he was still doing them.

One evening, I came in from work, and I was walking through the living room to my bedroom. My mom, her boyfriend, and his brother were sitting there, watching porn on TV. I walked past them, and my mom grabbed my arm and said, "You need to watch this." When I looked to see that they were watching porn, I told her, "I am tired, and that is nasty. I am not going to watch it." She grabbed me, forced me to sit by her, and held me there. I closed my eyes because it was so gross. When she let go of me a little, I broke free of her grasp, ran to my room, and locked the door. I could hear the TV and the three of them talking. I got dressed for bed, climbed in, and put the pillow over my head (trying not to hear what was coming from the next room). I was so tired from going to school and then straight to my job that it didn't take long for me to fall asleep.

The next thing I knew, I heard someone walking into my room and felt someone getting on top of me. I knew it was not my mom because this person was big and heavy. I woke up to find him (the brother) on top of me. I tried to get him off of me, but he was a stout guy. He covered my mouth and started tearing my clothes. He laughed and told me I was his now. I tried to kick him between the legs, but I couldn't. Before I knew it, he was inside me. I was trying to scream, and I was hitting him. Hitting him didn't faze him. He was rough and was groping me and laughing. It felt as if he were tearing my insides out. There was such heaviness and pressure inside. Feeling something run down my legs and hearing him moan in satisfaction made me just want to die. I was losing all sense of time and energy to fight. He smirked at me when I couldn't fight him anymore. The enjoyment he got out of it made me sick as he held me down against my will and did what he wanted to me. I wished I was dead then.

I asked God to take me, but this man had his way with me and held me where I could not get away. I heard someone else come into the room as I tried to scream for help. My brother had come in, grabbed the bat, and hit him across the back. He rolled off me, and he ran when my brother began hitting him with the bat. I ran to the bathroom in my room and locked it. I fell into the corner. I was so scared, and I cried. I fell asleep in the bathroom that night, and my brother stayed in the room to make sure he didn't come back.

The next day, I went to my mom and told her, "Your boyfriend's brother raped me last night."

She said, "I told you if you were to lose your virginity, it would be on my terms and not yours!"

I was so shocked that I almost fell to the ground. I know my eyes were wide as those of a deer caught in the headlights. I couldn't believe what I had just heard. I became angrier while looking at her. I just wanted to kill her. I yelled, "You had no right! How dare you!" I ran to my room, shut the door, and locked it when I saw it had been fixed. I assumed my brother fixed it for me. He was gone before I had gotten up that morning.

The events of that night were never brought up or spoken of between us. I was so angry at my mother and would give her evil looks and show my hatred toward her, even though it made things worse for me. She would smirk at me when she looked at me after that. At that point, I didn't care, and I just wished she would kill me. I knew then that it was better for my life to be snuffed out than to live in this empty body that was just a shell. Depression and hatred invaded my mind and soul. That was the moment I had no care, trust, or feeling left for anyone, not even for myself.

Brother, You Left Me

I was so excited when you came
Catching up
And all the games
You've been gone for so long
With your new life
I lost my heart's song
The pain I endured
While you were gone
I felt so alone
You were here for a little while
Before you went home
I hope you can see my lifestyle
As you see her beating me
The she-devil
She has become to me
I only ask this one thing
I beg of you
Don't leave me here with this thing
You begin to leave
And I cry
And I plead
I won't be a burden to you
I will leave everything behind
Just give me the clue
You have seen what she does to me
Let this be my solemn plea
Take me with you, brother
In this world
There can be no other
As I watch you leave
My heart stops

I feel my life leave me
I always thought we
Would be together
Then I guess our love
Was not strong enough
Now my life really sucks

My brother and I always got along. Not to say we didn't have our little spats. When we were kids, he always got me in trouble for things he did, but I always loved him. As we got older, we always hung out, and he loved me in his own way. He found his soulmate, and I was so happy for him.

My brother had his own challenges. When he was nineteen years old, he was in a car wreck that almost killed him, and he lost his left leg and foot below the knee. It devastated him. He had to learn how to talk again and was like a baby in a grown man's body. I went to school and stayed at the hospital at night to be there for him. It was a hard time that year, and even harder for him. I remember when he lived around the corner from us. He had met his girlfriend at the time. He had a car and was preparing to go to Mississippi with our dad. I begged him to take me with them and not leave me there. I was willing to leave everything and just take some clothes. He wouldn't take me with them, even though he had seen how our mother treated me. I was so upset and alone again. They left the next week, and all I could do was cry because I knew what was going to happen.

I died a little more that day. He left and left me there alone with our mother. Just to say I was right, it all got worse, and everything happened more often. She was mad because he left and took it out on me. She blamed me for him leaving and hated me even more. My brother was her baby, and in her eyes, he could do no wrong. He was in and out of jail for stuff he did, and she would always stand up for him even though she knew he did it and get him out of it.

Needless to say, it was not good for him. He was still my brother no matter what, and I always loved him. Seeing him today and the choices he has made do make me sad. I have never been able to talk to him about the day he left. I have forgiven him, but it hurts me so much. He has so many medical problems now, and he has had two strokes. I have not talked to him in a long time because of things that have happened and the choices he has made. I have had to distance myself from him. It will always remain the same, no matter what. I will always love him.

Mirror

I look into the mirror
I see a stranger
But I know it's me
As I see the flesh
The different shapes
It only reflects
When I look real deep
I see a kind soul
Who only wants to be loved
Eyes so dark
Full of emotions you can't see
A heart that beats
And feels like everyone else
I look into the mirror
I feel ashamed
I realize I am not the same
I am so ever different
It comes to me, I am happy
Though my flesh has faults
My personality, I have no second thoughts

They say the mirror tells no lies. It gives a reflection of what is and what is not and the deception of what could have been. As I look in the mirror, I see a person who is no longer me. The eyes are so dark with pain and hurt. There is a heart that beats but does not feel. Looking at this body before me, it has scars and is so pale. I stand looking at this girl who just wants to be loved by someone.

Just for once, I wish for someone to truly love me from the heart. Looking at this tattered body, I know no one wants this. I look at the scars from the inside out and say to myself, *You are not worth anything. No one wants a girl who has been beaten in body and soul.*

Where is my soul? I keep looking so hard to find mine in the mirror, but it is nowhere to be found. The mirror tells the truth about what you see on the outside. I ask myself, *Can it tell me what's on the inside?* Looking into this piece of glass, there reflects the flesh of a girl who no longer knows who she is. I am looking and thinking of all the wrong things with me. The face of a girl who used to be happy but now cannot tell you what that word means; a girl who longs for her mother to love her and no longer hates her; a girl who looks in this mirror and wonders what she did so badly to deserve this life of hell. That is what I see.

Personality—what is that? I don't know, but I only do what I have been trained to do. I can't have a personality of my own. I feel like a robot here, only to serve and deserve nothing in return. Mirror on the wall, do I deserve to stand or fall? Time went and came, and now I can't even look in the mirror anymore.

The Green Goblin

Green goblin, here you are
Always here
But never far
You can't stand me at all
No matter what
You like seeing me fall
Every little thing I do
Why are you angered?
I have no clue
When others see your
True face
Surprised and don't know what to do
If I do something
Even if we are together
You always have to do something better
You tell me you are tired
Of people doing for me
But against me, you conspire
Go away and leave me alone
Stay away
I don't like the goblin tone

They say the green goblin is the worst of all. This, I can confirm. What is a green goblin? He/she is jealous of another person or their life. This can cause all kinds of problems. My mom was such a green goblin toward me, especially as I got older. She would always tell me, "I don't know why people do things for you and won't do things for me." I didn't understand why either. I just always tried to treat people the way I wanted to be treated. My grandparents taught me that. If I did something for someone, she would try to outdo me to get more applause. I never wanted to be the center of attention. I always tried to help without expecting anything. When someone would tell me that I did a good job, it would make her so angry. When we would get home, it would be beating time.

I remember a time when we went to church (and I loved that church). There was a preacher who visited from out of town. At the end of the service, he prayed and prophesied over people. I went up for prayer, and of course, she jumped up and went too. The preacher prayed over me, and I could feel the Holy Spirit come over me. He went and prayed for her, but I noticed he did not touch her but prayed far from her instead. This angered her, and before she left, he told her in front of everyone, "You have been praying and praying, and God says he has heard you. There is something you are doing that is against him and his child. This needs to stop, or your life will become torture, and you will lose everything."

She was so angry, and I could tell by her face. She walked back and sat in the pew. As I was walking back, the preacher called me back up. He asked my name, and I told him it's Wendy. He said, "Wendy, God has great plans for you, and the day will come that you will be a walking Bible of God. You will be able to quote him word for word. He has amazing plans for you. Just keep your faith, pray, and live for him. Live for no one else, and no matter what happens, look to God and never give in to the darkness that is trying to take you. God has his plan, and in his time, you will become that plan and become his disciple." (You know I forgot about this, but it is amazing how God reminds you.)

So when we left (this is how the green goblin works), we got in the car, and she peeled out in the parking lot and flew down the road.

I asked her to please slow down because I was so scared. She just said, "I am tired of you getting everything. That was supposed to be for me. I was supposed to get a prophecy, not you!"

I asked her to pull over, and she finally did. I tried to get out of the car, and as I began to step out, she gassed it, and the door slammed on my leg. She said, "You want out, I will let you out permanently!"

When I looked up, she was heading straight for a telephone pole. I screamed, "Stop! Please stop! God, please help me." She swerved just in time and missed it.

When we got home, I jumped out of the car, ran into my room, and locked my door. I cried and prayed as she stood outside my door, yelling, "Next time, I won't miss! You remember that." I never slept that night. Her cruelty and darkness, combined with her green goblin attitude, were so frightening, and it scared me to death. I couldn't believe a mother could be so cruel to her child. When the green goblin would appear, my heart would stop, not knowing what she would do next. God knows I just crept into my own world to try to leave that one.

CHAPTER 4

Nothing More

Many of One

Here we go again
She has her claws in a man
He has fallen for her charm
But she plans only more harm
One, two, three
How many will it be?
Just as evil as she
Why does it have to be?
The sin of both
Neither to say no
Dealing with one but now two
How do I elude?
One pain, one same
Is double afar
She says, he says
Just let me lie dead
The look of dispute of one or two
How can love come
From me to you?
Here one minute, gone the next
Not knowing what the context
One more bites the dust
Another one with lust

Marriage—if you asked what I thought about it when I was younger, I would have said, "Marriage is not for me." Why, you say? Because my mom has been married so many times, and all of them failed. There was abuse between them, or the man was abusing me. They were either alcoholics or drug heads. I remember there were only two who were good; they were my dad and my stepdad Darian. I cannot remember much of my dad, but I do remember Darian. Darian was a sweet guy, and he treated me like his own daughter. My mom was so mean, though. I remember him serving in the navy on submarines. He wound up with diabetes and was honorably discharged. Even after he divorced her, he still came and took me places and treated me like his own. When he eventually left her, he made a promise to me that he would always be around, and he kept that promise until he got sick with bone cancer, and that just ate him up.

I went to see him all the time because they had to put him in Life Care, a hospice facility. I remember the day I received the phone call that he was about to die. I hurriedly left work and was on my way to the nursing home. When I got there, they said he would pass soon, and I asked if I could see him. The doctor told me that there was one other thing. They could not get his eyes closed, and he was barely breathing. It was as if he was waiting for something to take his last breath.

I went in by myself and sat on the bed beside him and said, "Dad, I am here now. I love you, and you will always be in my heart. I will miss you so much, but I know you will not be far away, and there will be no more pain for you. Dad, I will be okay, and you can go home now. Tell everyone I said hello." At that moment, he squeezed my hand, smiled, and took his last breath. I knew he was gone, and I closed his eyes, kissed his forehead, and said, "I love you." This man meant so much to me. He was the only man who told me that I was strong and to never give in.

Wow, I still miss him to this day, but I know he is dancing and watching over me. For all the other men she dated or married, they were evil like she was, and sometimes worse. She was a woman who used them, and they used her. She thought she couldn't do without a man. She didn't want to work and expected everyone else to pay her way. The men didn't stay long; they grew tired of her, of us. I remember being yelled at and slapped by many of them and being treated like a slave. Instead of one devil, I had two.

Where Are You?

Where are you?
I have no clue
You say you are close
But I see no escape rope
You say you love me
You say you will set me free
I can't see you
So why should I believe in you?
You gave me to a woman
Who does not want me
She is cruel and insane
For everything, I am to blame
I feel as though you have abandoned me
Are you ashamed of me?
They say you are the creator
That nothing else matters
That you are the everlasting maker
Did you forget me?
Will you free me?
I have prayed for you to save me
I am still enslaved to her
Why do you leave me here?
I bet you are not even near
Why won't you save me?
Maybe it is true what she claims to me
That you don't want me either
Even though you are the creator
I do as I am told
I am not bold
I try to be strong, but it won't be long
Maybe I was a mistake
God, where are you?
I don't know how much more I can take

As time passes, your mind begins to roam. Going to church, you hear that God is the creator of all things and that he will see you through. Believing that seems far from the truth to me. For I knew God had left me.

I prayed, and everything was still the same day after day. The routine feeling of death upon me prevented me from feeling as if God was interested in what was going on in my life. Living with a person who is supposed to love you and see you through life but realizing that person hates you with every fiber of her being makes you wonder why God created you and gave you to such a cruel person.

No matter what I did for her, it was never enough to please her. I felt like I was being punished for just being born, and I did not know why I was enslaved to a master who would never free me. I wondered that if God was so mighty, then why hadn't he freed me from this cruel woman? I could not understand why I had to be here. I had anxiety and depression. I wanted to just die. In my mind, God was so far away that he just didn't care and had better things to do than worry about me. She would tell me that God did not love me, and I began believing her as the darkness began to take over. I felt I would not be able to take it anymore, at least not much longer. I just felt so alone and had no one to turn to. Where was I to go? Or would I ever get out?

Take Me

Another day is here
Little faith, some fear
Body full of scars
Wished I was far away as Mars
My eyes open again
As another day begins
Why do I still breathe?
Just let me be free
I don't want to think
I'm so on the brink
To look at all the scars
Do I have flesh or tar?
I can't see myself in the mirror
The darkness is nearer
I can't deal with another breath
I can feel my soul coming to death
No more
Just come TAKE ME

I am waking up to another day of pain and hate. My faith is depleting, and more fear is creeping in. Looking at my body and seeing scars that should not be there, I wish I were just so far away from here and this earth. I wonder why I have awakened to another day and why I just can't die in my sleep. I don't want to look at my scarred body and just hang on with a thread. I wish I could just stop breathing. My soul dies little by little, and it's like I am invisible in the mirror when I look at myself. The breath feels like it is not even my own. My soul is dying and disappearing. Looking in the mirror and seeing the darkness in my eyes, it is unmistakable that my heart is full of sorrow and pain. I feel like my skin is tarred from all the pain and blackness from the brushes and cuts.

God, just take me! Take me to where there is no more pain! In this life, it is so not worth it.

My Anger

As my mind wanders into the deep
Of all the darkness
My thoughts go wild
To no light
Deep, deep into the darkness
The anger comes up slowly
As I feel it travel
Through my skin and veins
So much I can feel myself
Fixing to explode
Not knowing what I might do or where I will go
The fire burns in my heart so hot
That you can't touch
As I feel my face turn red
My heart beats fast
My chest can't stand the pain
My mind is gone
My thoughts of hatred
The evil forms in me
All my mind can wrap around
Is how I can hurt you
It clouds my mind
To me, there is no sense of time
No cares and no worries
No cares about the consequences
All I know is what I feel
And no way to control the anger

Anger! I did not realize how deep it could go. The deepest cuts and scars, no matter how you try to hide them, seem to creep up when least expected. Anger toward everything and everyone. The least little thing turns it on, and it's hard to shut it off. It creeps its way up. There is a burning sensation of veins popping and exploding. Every time she hit, slapped, cut, or even choked me, my anger would become more and more dangerous.

First, my mind did not recognize it, and later, when it happened, I could feel it. My heart would start racing, and I could feel it pounding in my chest. My mind would seem to just disappear into the darkness, and all I could think about was how I was going to hurt her. I could feel my blood racing through my body. In my veins, it felt like fire from a volcanic eruption flowing through at a racing pace. I could feel the anger building up around me, just traveling like a snake through every inch of my skin. The darkness would take me over, inch by inch. My head would pound like a drum, and thoughts of evil would run all around. My skin would feel so tight, like I was about to burst right out of it!

An explosion of mass destruction would form as I felt the darkness take over and get stronger with each rush. It felt as if someone else was in my body, taking over my mind and soul—as if my soul had been buried and someone else's thoughts were my own. I had no cares of what would become of me as the darkness was telling me, "Do it! It's what you want." Somewhere, I could feel myself fighting to come back up to the surface. One voice was fighting to tell me not to do it, but the darkness surrounding me choked the other's voice away. It was such a raging feeling in my soul, and the littlest thing could set it off. The anger was just sitting and waiting to show its face. I never knew how it would show its face, or what might make it come out—a word said, a gesture made, or a body motion. A word that was said could start a chain reaction. I had a constant battle just to tame the beast within. Anger could be found hiding in the shadow, a corner, or a vein.

One Shot

As I lie in my bed
Thoughts are running in my head
What should I do?
I have no clue
The scars are real
Time is never still
The anger sits and boils
There is only one recoil
I have one shot
It's the perfect shot
Walking through the darkness
But I can't miss
Enter at my own risk
This will be my last wish
Take the shiny gun
Don't you dare run
Point it straight ahead
Stand beside the bed
Come on, one bullet to the head
While lying asleep in the bed
No more pain, laughter, torture, or shame
No more darkness, for she is to blame
No more scars, blood, or bruises
No more puppet or slave
To be free is what I crave
Just pull the trigger
Put it nearer
As my hands shake
I begin to think, *This is a mistake*
I know she will become awaken
How can I take a life?
Even though she has put me in so much strife

What will I gain? Just more pain
So maybe it's not one shot but maybe two
So I don't have to live
So there won't be a misgive
My soul says yes
My heart says no
Which one do I control?
The choice is mine
I only have this one time
Today I still live
My heart won, and no shots from the gun

So much was going on in my mind. I was at my wit's end and knew no one—not even God—was going to save me. How was I to try to get myself out of the situation when I just wanted to die anyway? Then the idea came to me. Like an answer to my prayers. I could not stop thinking about it all day, especially as the day went by and she had her usual beat-me party.

That night, I locked myself in my room and cried, knowing that this was the only answer and that it would be over soon. When she finally went to sleep, I tiptoed to her room. Standing there, I listened to see if she was awake. Not hearing anything, I slowly opened the door. Seeing her sleeping like a baby, I instantly felt rage looking at her and thought, *How could she sleep knowing what she has been doing?*

I crept to her dresser, opened it, and moved her clothes. I saw what I was looking for. I heard that voice saying, "This is the only way to be free. Do it!" I picked up the .25 pistol and looked at it as if it were the only thing in the world left to free me. I loaded it quietly and walked to the side of her bed. Thoughts were running through my head. *She will never let you go. You will be her slave forever. She will beat you every day, and you will suffer, and no one will help you!* I stood there, wondering and hoping she would not wake up. I looked at her sleeping so peacefully, and I knew that was all I wanted—peace.

I began pointing the gun at her head. I said, "My freedom is worth more to me than you, and now I will be forever free of you with no more pain." I was amazed that she did not wake up because, usually, the least little thing would wake her. As I was about to pull the trigger, I could feel the anger engulf me. I felt relieved at the same time. Right then, before the gun went off and before I pulled the trigger all the way, I heard a voice say, "No," really loudly in my head. It was so loud that it hurt my head, and I let go of the trigger. I knew that when I shot her, I would pull the gun on myself so there would be no more pain. The voice again said, "No, not this way!" It was as if I were frozen in time and could not move. I felt as if someone was in the room with me, but I knew no one was there. I could feel another presence there. It was as if someone were guiding me as I unloaded the gun and put it back in the same place she had it. It was exactly in the same spot, and I left the room.

That night, I cried quietly in my room so as not to wake her. I did not understand what had happened. All I knew was that I was still alive, and so was she. Saddened and just done, I knew that, for some reason, I had been stopped from my mission. Not knowing why or what was in store for me, all I could do was cry and call out to God, "Why am I still alive?" Not receiving an answer or knowing just made it worse. Did I really know and just couldn't see the answer? My life then was just being the hamster in the wheel.

C H A P T E R   5

The Unimaginable

Heavenly Grace

You were there when I needed you
With your love
I happily greeted you
When I thought I couldn't go anymore
You reached for me
Your graceful hand pulled me ashore
When my heart ached with pain
Your love filled me up and still remains
When I sinned over again
I begged for forgiveness
You forgave again, and again
When I cried at night, you came
And held me lovingly tight
When I reached out to you
You smiled so beautifully
You took my hand
I pray I may stay in your grace
Forevermore
You took me to your heavenly place
And there is where I will wish
That when the day comes, I will stay

There were so many trials, and days were full of me just wanting to disappear, but you wouldn't let me. Just as I felt as if I couldn't take another breath, it seemed as if you gave me more air to breathe. As time came and went, it was as though you were working for me, but I couldn't see it. I prayed more and put everything into it. I felt the Holy Spirit surrounding me as if to let me know everything would be okay. I messed up. I didn't get rid of the hate I was feeling, but you forgave me. I felt like a failure.

During the day of darkness, I felt a little awakened. I felt that somehow I knew you were there but didn't know how to get to you. When I cried that night, I felt as if I could feel you wrap your arms around me and comfort me. I tried so hard, but reality kept hitting me in the flesh and in my thoughts. I would imagine you smiling at me and letting me know you were there, and I would be forgiven. The combination of pain from reality and emotions was overwhelming at times, and all I could do was cry.

I dreamed of you reaching out to me with the biggest smile. I felt the peace, love, and joy as you reached for me. I dreamed of leaving this world and of you taking me by the hand and leading me to heaven! Being in your grace and presence was amazing! The peace and love I felt were soothing. I wanted to just stay there in your presence, but I realized I would wake up on earth. I would keep dreaming this dream, and every time, it was the same but different, as if you were trying to tell me something I couldn't understand.

One day, I know I will know you completely and be the woman you want for me.

How Do I Find You?

All that has been
All that is seen
Life I live
Through everything
I look here
I look there
But you are nowhere
No idea where you are
Search high and low
Search my house
Search my car
Search on my phone
Where are you?
I look at myself
And wonder
the wonders of where you can be
I look in the mirror
Can you be me?
Do I pray to see you?
Do I read your words?
To find you!
When I cry, do you come?
Where can you be?
I just don't know how to see
How do I find you?

How do I find you? I do not understand. I have these continuing doubts about whether you are even there. I looked everywhere just to see any sign of you in reality. I looked in my car and house to see if I could feel your presence, but nothing. Is it me who can't feel you, or am I looking over you? I looked at my phone and saw all the Christian posts and inspirational quotes. There is nothing! Why can't I find any sign of you? Are you hiding from me, or have I shamed you again? I am wondering, Are you hiding in me so I can't see you? I wonder: If I read your word, will you be standing before me? Or am I just blind to you? Why will you hide from me? The thoughts run through my head.

The voices say you hide and are no longer near. Lord, where are you? How do I find you and your grace? How do I find your presence in my life? I looked in the mirror, and I just saw an empty shell, and I can't see your love anywhere. Sometimes when I cry, I can't feel you! Is it because I cry so much that I can't find you? Are you tired of hearing me weep? Can you hear my pain or place your eyes on it? How do I find you, Lord, and why do you seem to be a ghost to me? Are you my shadow or just invisible?

When I look in the mirror, I just see an empty soul. They say the Holy Spirit is in every person, but I think mine has left me. I heard that the Holy Spirit is light, but I only see darkness. How can I get out of this life that is my hell? How bad I must have been for you to stay away from me?

Take It

Take my money
Take my possessions
Take my kindness as if it were funny
Let me see
Let me be
Let you see the hurt in me
Beat my soul
Beat my flesh
Beat my name until I don't know it
As you take a piece here
As you take a piece there
It will not get you anywhere
Break my bones
Break my heart
Breaking all is known
Say you're sorry
Say never again
Say it again tomorrow
Day after day
Hour after hour
Knowing it's coming again tomorrow
Through all the pain
Through all the tears
What was there to gain?
You thought you won
You thought I was broken
Your thoughts were spoken
Today I stand
Today I live
All the years I'd been mending
Just to say I did not stay
Now you are a memory and
You have gone away

So you want it all! So just take it! You can take my money, possessions, and kindness as if you are not concerned. A mother who thinks she is entitled to everything. I wish you would just let me be. You can see how you are hurting me, but you don't have a care in the world. As you beat my flesh and soul, you just make me hollow. As if you care about all the demons in your air.

The constant beatings, choking, and cruelty—you just kept them going, trying to break my bones and my soul. You came back to me and said you were sorry, but you didn't mean it. You turned around and did it again. You were not getting your way, and then you came back slaying. Seeing the pain, hiding the tears, and knowing the fear—where has it gotten you?

Years of cruelty were so unimaginable. There was nothing else to gain but hatred from me. You thought you were breaking me down, but you did not know that my spirit was fighting every step of the way. You always said what you thought of me, and you held no words back. Through it all, I still stood, not knowing how or why. I was still alive, not knowing how strong I had become.

I am still breathing, away from you. There is no more hurt or pain. I have forgiven you, but I have dusted my feet off you. You are still mean and cruel, though you are just a memory of my past that made me strong for the future. I think of you no more, as if you were wiped from my mind. A distance so far away, there just to make me remember what I have survived.

CHAPTER 6

The Way Beyond

My Precious Gift

As I leave the doctor
And in such a shock
I find a gift
A little life in me
I cry in excitement
And I fear too
But know you are a gift
From God too
My mind is racing
And I am pacing
Knowing you are a treasure
As my heart has pleasure
Praying to God to know
And knowing you will grow
Scared to be on my own
Thinking how I am going to raise you
And not fail you
All these thoughts in the beginning
Makes my head go swimming
As I sit in the chair
Knowing not really in despair
Praying to God for answers
Getting my thoughts together
Knowing you are my treasure
Ready to make it through the weather
My choice was a no-brainer
There was no retainer
My gift from God
My precious child
My life is forever changed
In every great way.

At the age of thirty-seven, your body changes, and your internal clock is ticking! I was with a man for almost two years. A man who I loved very much. A man who had cheated, whom I had forgiven and wanted to spend my life with. A man who made me feel good and was good to me. Someone who knew some of my past. Someone I thought I could talk to and share everything with. Not knowing what God had for me.

My menstrual cycle was never regular from the time I started, and I never knew when I would have them or how long they would last. Many times, I would go from seven days to a month. I wouldn't have anything for two to three months. It was so crazy. Being told you can't have children because of the abuse was mind-blowing and crushing at the same time. When you are told news like this, it sends you into a dark zone even more.

I often wondered if this was my punishment for something I did and if God was not pleased with me. Did God think I didn't deserve a child? Why was life so cruel when all I wanted was a child to love and love me back? Eventually, I accepted my faith and lived life the best I could. Being with the man I was with, I felt loved in ways I never knew were possible, and I experienced life. There were ups and downs, just like in everything, but we never argued, fussed, or fought. I never had a clue! My breasts started hurting. I wasn't on my menstruation period, which was the norm, but they were extra sore, and it felt weird.

I remembered calling my sister because she is a nurse, and I told her what was going on. She asked, "Have you taken a pregnancy test?" I am not going to lie. That really shocked me. She asked about my cycle and if it was still messed up. I was like, "Yes," and she said, "Just try it and see." So I went to the store and bought two pregnancy tests. I called to tell her I had them, and she proceeded to tell me how to do it.

So the next morning, I did as she said, and when it was time to look at it, there were two pink lines. (So I thought to myself, *No way! This thing has to be wrong.*) The next morning, I did the second test. Lo and behold, there were two pink lines. I immediately called my sister and told her the results. She told me to make an appointment with my doctor because the test can be wrong and just to make sure and take the extra step of certainty.

I made an appointment for my doctor. The appointment came. I was so scared. I was beside myself and didn't know what to do or where my thoughts were going. My hands were sweaty and numb. The nurse called me and gave me a cup and said, "Pee in it." I went to the restroom and did what she said. I came back and gave her the cup. They told me to sit in the room and that the doctor would be in shortly. I felt butterflies floating in my stomach. The doctor came in and said, "Hello, Ms. Kinsey."

I said, "Hello."

He proceeded to tell me, "Do you want the good news or the bad news first?"

That really scared me. I told him, "Give me the bad first."

The doctor then said, "Well, the doctors were wrong!"

My heart dropped to my feet. I could feel it go right down.

"The good news is that you are pregnant."

I literally passed out!

I remember waking up on a bed and wondering if it was all a dream. The doctor said, "Ms. Kinsey, you okay?"

I told him he was fibbing and asked, "Is this a joke?"

He then requested the nurse bring in the test and my pee sample. She did, and then he said, "The nurse will dip the tester in your pee, and if it turns pink, it means you are pregnant."

I watched her dip it and waited for a minute. She came over to me to show me and explained, "If it is bright pink, you're pregnant. If white, you are not."

When she showed the test to me, it was as pink as pink can get!

The doctor said, "You are about two months pregnant."

I could feel my mouth drop and my tongue roll right on out like a red-carpet event.

The doctor then asked, "You didn't notice any changes this time?"

I told him, "No, I have not gotten sick at all and no unusual cycles, just my normal."

So he said he would schedule an ultrasound and checkups and that he would have to keep a close eye on me because I was at high risk.

I left, went to my car, and called my boyfriend. I told him I needed to talk to him. He said, "Yes," and that he would be there.

When I got there, we came out on the porch, and I told him I was pregnant. He got mad, and he told me, "I told you I didn't want any more kids."

I replied, "I showed you my medical records and said I could not get pregnant because of the abuse!"

He then said, "What are you going to do now?"

I said, "What do you mean?"

He said, "Are you going to have an abortion or give it up for adoption?"

I could not believe my ears. This was a miracle. I know God gave me this, and my boyfriend just didn't care about this life we created together. I told him, "I will not do either one. Have you lost your mind? This is a miracle that God has given me!"

He said, "Then we are done, and I will not take part in it."

I was broken, and I left. Driving home, I cried so hard. When I got home, I decided that I would do this on my own and raise my baby no matter what. I would do what I had to. It was a hard pregnancy. I was always at the doctor's office for appointments, and I lost my job because of my pregnancy. I had to move in with my sister and then get a place.

I remember hurting and calling for an appointment.

When I got there, I told them the baby was coming, and they thought it was Braxton-Hicks pains. A nurse hooked me up to the machine and went to do something. When she came back and looked at the machine, she ran back out and came back with a wheelchair. She said, "Ms. Kinsey, I called the hospital. They are expecting you and will check you into your room."

The van was waiting when we got outside, and they took me across the street to the hospital and checked me in. I was in the room, and I called my dad. He didn't want to come, so I called my sister. She came right up. She stayed with me the whole time. She has always been my angel. When the time came, the baby was ready. It took twelve hours or more for him to be born. There were complications, like when they lost his heartbeat and had to stick a wire into his head to look inside and make sure he was okay. I couldn't take any pain medicine because my platelets were low. They had to break my water, and he came flying out!

I saw his face looking at me, and he was so quiet. Seeing my beautiful boy, I was so amazed. My sister brought him over to me, but the doctor said I couldn't hold him because he ripped me all the way down and I was bleeding badly. They stitched me up and finally gave me morphine for pain. I was out for the whole day. When I woke up, they brought him to me. I cried because he was so beautiful. I kissed his head and held him, never wanting to let him go. I have raised him ever since on my own. My sister helped when she could. He is smart and handsome, and he is my pride and joy.

As I Come Together

My mind is here
My body is there
My soul is still nowhere
The more I read
Your word works in me
I begin to have faith
Just a little I take
Because you say
Enough as a mustard seed
As I read your word
It throws me a curve
As I pray
I can feel you stay
I feel you near me
As the water in the sea
My thoughts change
I feel I have more to gain
As I start to feel safe
Each and every day
My heart feels a calm weather
As I think I am
Coming together

Having your mind in so many places at once can drive you crazy.

My mind was here and there, thinking about everything. Memories came back to haunt me, but I tried to push them away.

It's when your body wants to go somewhere else and just stay. My body gives me one signal, and my mind another. It's so confusing.

I started reading the Bible, which is your Word, and I understood what it meant. Each word I read had a different meaning to me, and more emotions emerged. As I read more, my faith began to grow, and my eyes began to see. I saw that your words could make me closer to you. As thoughts of what you said made me realize what you have given so I could live, I felt as if you healed me by your Word as I read the love you gave. I started to try to pray but did not know what to say. As I prayed, tears came out like a river, and they did not seem to stop. I felt relief as the emotions and hurt came out. I prayed that you would give me strength.

I prayed for my soul and for the hate in my heart to eventually leave. My heart felt calm as my life began, and I knew the pain of waking up every day was going to be gone from me. I prayed I could learn to trust anyone who came across my path, but I knew deep down that I couldn't. I was just taking one step at a time and knew that with each breath, I could live. As the days went by, I learned to pray with more conviction, not to ask for myself but for others. My heart became free and calm in my thoughts of the future. My faith seemed to grow more and more in so many ways.

God says to have faith like a mustard seed. This faith is so small, but it is so real. Lord, I've started to feel you closer to me now in everything I do and everywhere I go.

What's My Purpose?

Purpose of life
As it's defined
In every strife
What is my purpose?
As I wonder
Day in and day out
To whom is it worth
Some say nothing
Some say something
As my mind wonders
In every thought
Every area of my life
The pain and trials
The hurt and scars
Weeping, depression, anger
Not knowing where I belong
Trying to fit in but
Still being an outcast
Why do I have to be alone?
The whispers and glances
The laughter on my way
Wanting nothing but love
Getting nothing but grief
Getting knocked down, getting back up again
My body and soul
So bruised and battered
Who would want me?
So I asked, What is my purpose?

Have you ever wondered why you were created? Why are you here? I have many times. I have had so much strife in my life. There has been pain by flesh and emotions. Shame and hate fill my emotions. I have heard people talk about destiny and purpose. I have always wondered what mine would have been in this life on earth. Some people say your purpose is worth everything, and some don't believe in it. I don't know what it would be like for me.

As I think of everything that happened in my life—so much hurt in my soul and heart, pain in my flesh and bones, so many scars on my body—I am reminded of what I have been through in life. I shed tears of pain and depression that were creeping into my mind. At times, I do not want to be around others. The anger dwells in me and triggers more that came. I tried to be like others to fit in, not knowing who I am. I tried the things that others do, but I did not feel like myself. Though I tried, other people still treated me as an outcast. People whispered, laughed, and giggled as I walked by. I wondered if they were laughing at me.

I felt their eyes follow me as I went by, and it made me wonder if I had something on me. I was treated as if I did not matter or that I was just for show for others. When I get knocked down, I get back up, dust myself off, and keep going. I did this constantly. It was so tiring for me. I just wanted to quit sometimes and not deal with anything.

My body and soul are so bruised and battered in such a manner that I don't know where I will be next. So who knows what my purpose is, where it is to take place, or how it is to happen? Who knows my purpose in life as I live it every day? Is purpose an action you take or a change in life that is better than the life you have now? So what is your purpose?

The Child in Me

My child who was born
So deeply in me
Who is never torn
Beauty as deep as the sea
Shines so brightly
Who never defies me
Who carries my name
With all but love
Who could never be of shame
She knows of my
Everlasting pain
For she feels me
But only has everlasting to gain
Feeling my anger
For she cannot help herself
For she is no stranger
Feeling the love of her Father
In so much beauty
For there is not another
For when she cries
Them crystal tears
For I feel my heart dies
I feel my children's sadness
For it bears my soul
For I know she can feel my madness
For when she rejoices in me
That beautiful voice
It so pleases thee
For I talk through her the magnificent sound
That cannot be curved
For when time ends
My ever-loving child
You will fix all amends

For you are blessed
Never to be harmed
For this, I confess
For your deeds time seven
Child of mine
I await you in heaven
So be pure of heart
My chosen one
For be overly smart
Give my words free
May they all ring
And pray they may all conceive
My golden child of mine
With the power of life
May you forever shine.

People say, How does he talk to you? Well, it is different for everyone. As I began to live a life of freedom, God began to let me know how beautiful I was to him. I have always tried to ask God how I could be the person he meant for me to be. With the pains that I felt, I kind of knew what God went through, but not to the extent he had, just a little taste of it. I know his pain can never compare to anything on this earth. I knew he was the only Father I had who truly loved me through all of this life I had gone through.

I realized that when I cried, somehow I knew he was crying too. I slowly realized that I could be in his presence. I felt the Holy Ghost. I wanted to just sing with all my might to praise him. I realized that he had a destiny set for me, but I did not know what it was.

I know I am a good listener. When he told me I would bring the truth to others and help them with it, I wondered why and how. I realize I am his special child, as we all are. Knowing that someone knows my pain without saying anything is like a light shining through me. I pray that I do his will, and when the time comes, I will be with him, rejoicing in heaven. I want to be the one to whom he says, "My special child, you have done well and spoken the truth. I am well pleased."

CHAPTER 7

My Purpose

When you are in any relationship, no matter whether it is mother-daughter, son-mother, daughter-father, father-son, wife-husband, or girlfriend-boyfriend, the life you give is the life you live. Wow, the power in that statement. Can you imagine the life you have now and the life you can have in the future?

As a child, I couldn't have predicted that my life would turn out the way it did. The days of my life, from a baby to a child to a teenager to an adult—the times of hate fulfilled me, and depression wanted to take me to the darkness.

Everyone imagines their life being full of love, joy, and just peace, but not trauma, pain, flesh, or ripping agony. In life, there are many paths you can take, and there is always room to change. I was a child trying to please and do everything right—in the sense of the innocent mind and spirit. Realizing that you cannot please everyone person on earth makes you wonder, *Is it me?* Growing up in a broken home, there was a lot of pain, and no love was given. When you give so much of yourself and just stay in a toxic relationship, the cycle is never-ending.

I learned as I got older that nothing my mother did was going to change. I was not given the chance to live my life, especially knowing that she had purposely had me raped and had such hatred for me. The beatings and her choking me until I was unconscious were her ways of controlling me. She threatened to kill me in my sleep and locked me up in my room as a child. I remember I was so scared and would hide in the closet or under my bed, praying she would not find me. After being raped, I lost all sense of myself, and it was as if I were someone else. I became sexually active with the guy I was dating and had no care. It was as if I were a robot with no feelings. I didn't date anymore as I got older and trusted no one. I didn't trust men or women, no matter who they were.

I became a hermit and didn't associate much. I just closed myself off from the world. I slowly began to trust certain people, but in my mind, once you hurt me, the wall went up, and you couldn't get back in. I never found out why my mother did what she did to me, and I probably will never find out.

Today, I am fine with that. As I learn more about myself and learn to trust and love again, it's becoming clearer why I went through everything I did. God had his plans for me, and all my life has been a setup to make me the strong woman I am today.

In learning to trust God, I am also learning to trust people again. I've learned to show the love that God equipped me with and show compassion, no matter what. What has changed my perspective on everything? You know, if you had told me before that God had a plan for me, I would have angrily said, "What? To give me pain?" But in a sense, that pain has taught me what no man or woman could show me at that moment. No matter what emotions controlled me at the time, I never gave up on God. I always had the faith of a mustard seed.

Today, I realize my purpose is to fulfill my North Star and his purpose for me. To give love, truth, honor, joy, light, and God's Word to those who need them. My heart is full of the love of God, who has prepared me for my purpose-filled life. God gives us grace and love because he is grace and love. I want to leave you with this thought.

What is your purpose? Are you in the right room that God has wanted you to step into? I know it can take your life, turn it upside down, and make you not live anymore. Take it from me. Don't give up. God was there with you and is there with you through it all. All you have to do is ask him to help and give you strength and courage. Ask him to fill you and stay with you. He will. I am living proof of his love, strength, and purpose. I am not saying it won't be hard, but fight like the CHAMPION that he made you to be. I am forty-six years old now, and my life is not over, nor is yours. No matter the age, grade, or concept, God will take you as you are, not as you are trying to be.

Take the leap of faith and see how God can change and mold you as he created you to be! We are all champions of God. Let us tell our stories and step into his grace and the abundance he has planned for us. It's time to take your weapon out (the Bible) and show the world your God and what he can do! Let your inner champion come out and shine through him! It is only in his love and the Holy Spirit that we can experience true freedom and life. A life of freedom is what we should all have.

I did not come to this point overnight, and God is still working for me today. Put him in your relationship, home, business, and children, and see what he can do for you. So if you can trust a man who has failed you, then why can't you trust God, who has not failed you? God has taken all my tears, pain, and hurt and turned them into joy, love, and peace.

If you can't trust what you don't see, think of it this way: When the wind blows, you feel it, but you can't see it, right? Why is God any different? We want to trust in the things on earth, but in the end, God created everything on it, so why not trust him?

God Turned Beauty from Ashes

In my life, I have had to struggle and have been through so much pain, madness, hurt, torture, and grief. If you look back, you can see that I was able to get away from it all with God's grace and mercy. He sent someone to take me out of the situation. Since I have been gone, I have learned to do for myself, love myself, love others, and live a life that I thought could never happen. God has guided me to make sure I stay on his path. I have had a chance to start a relationship with my father and my brother. My sister found me, and we have gotten to know each other and are the best of friends. My siblings and my dad have gotten to know me as a person and a woman of faith. I have grown in my faith in God, and believe me, it was hard at first. But now that I know myself, I can live the life that God meant for me.

I have moved several times, and I went back to school and got my GED. I went to college, received my criminal justice degree, and graduated with a 3.64 GPA. My son (literally my miracle child from God) was born in 2013. God saw me through having to raise my son as a single mother. When you think there is no way to pay bills or get the things you need for your child, think again.

I always prayed, and just as I began to think it was hopeless, God showed me otherwise. I am not saying I didn't have doubts. Of course, the devil fought me, but God won out. I never let go of him, no matter what I went through. God always puts me somewhere for a reason.

I met my now-husband in Oil City, Louisiana. We were friends for over a year. I was not looking for anyone because I had been with men for a long time who cheated. So we hung out as friends. To tell you the truth, I gave up on the idea because, at the age of forty-six years old, I thought I was just going to be alone. Actually, I was sort of okay with that, but I told the Lord I would give it to him. Not long after I did that, a wonderful man came to my son's birthday party, and I just can't explain it, but we clicked. It was as if lightning struck me.

God let me know that man was for me. We talked the whole time. After the birthday party, we talked on the phone a lot. I came to see him in Texas, and he came to see me. Not long after that, he proposed to me, and I said yes. I knew he was for me, and he told me he knew I was for him. You see, God put us together, and he knew what he was doing. My husband treats me like a queen, and he is a God-fearing man. God may not do what you want or pray for in your time, but he always does it in his time. I am a strong woman and a warrior of God now. Most of all, I am no longer a survivor. I am a CHAMPION of God!

A B O U T   T H E   A U T H O R

The true story of Wendy Sims's life from infancy to childhood and from teen to adult. The secret was kept, silenced, and denied until today. The awkwardness of abuse and trauma, even rape, are kept as secrets and never told in society. Wendy Sims was never taught differently and was too scared to say anything for fear of retaliation against her. She received threats against her life, if sh ever told. She felt trapped in the situation for a long time. Throughout her life, she has gone through tremendous pain and trauma and is still here today. She has survived a life that has sent her through the pit of fire and back. Today, Wendy Sims has made it through and found her strength and her purpose in her life. Now, Wendy Sims is out to fulfill her destiny that Jesus has for her in this life. According to Britannica, the definition of *child abuse* is *cruelty to children*. It is the willful infliction of pain and suffering on children through physical, sexual, or emotional mistreatment.